LET THE
LOVE-LIGHT IN

A Book Coming Forth to Lighten
Your Load of Sorry Nights and
Faulty Flights and Major Overload

STEFANIE FINN

BALBOA.
PRESS

A DIVISION OF HAY HOUSE

Balboa Press books may be ordered through booksellers or by contacting:

Balboa Press
A Division of Hay House
1663 Liberty Drive
Bloomington, IN 47403
www.balboapress.com
1 (877) 407-4847

Because of the dynamic nature of the Internet, any web addresses or
links contained in this book may have changed since publication and
may no longer be valid. The views expressed in this work are solely those
of the author and do not necessarily reflect the views of the publisher,
and the publisher hereby disclaims any responsibility for them.

The author of this book does not dispense medical advice or prescribe the
use of any technique as a form of treatment for physical, emotional, or medical
problems without the advice of a physician, either directly or indirectly. The
intent of the author is only to offer information of a general nature to help you
in your quest for emotional and spiritual well-being. In the event you use any
of the information in this book for yourself, which is your constitutional right,
the author and the publisher assume no responsibility for your actions.

Any people depicted in stock imagery provided by Thinkstock are
models, and such images are being used for illustrative purposes only.
Certain stock imagery © Thinkstock.

Print information available on the last page.

ISBN: 978-1-5043-8775-0 (sc)
ISBN: 978-1-5043-8776-7 (e)

Balboa Press rev. date: 09/19/2017

WHERE IS THIS BOOK FROM?

This book is from the planes of distant shores where Mighty Angels reside.

They've come to help the ones who find their way here now.

Stefanie is just the vessel through which our love has found your attention in this moment in which our love abounds.

Falter not in this desperate state of tired and shaky stead.

This information will be astounding if you let it penetrate your mind.

So open up and let it do what it's intended to.

This book contains the new codes coming forth to lighten up your load of sorry nights and faulty flights and major overload.

MESSAGE FROM STEFANIE

This book was written from start to finish in five days.

In early May of 2017, I began to experience something extraordinary happening to me.

While driving home following a spiritual retreat, I felt as though some kind of a portal had opened up at the crown of my head, and through it a feeling of tender bliss began flowing into my mind.

A few nights after I returned home, I told a friend that I felt as though I was on the precipice of something. I couldn't put my finger on it, but I knew something big was about to happen.

Then, on May 24, 2017, I woke up in the middle of the night in a way that I had been awakened hundreds of times over the past fifteen years - hearing a short message or a stream of thought. This night's stream started with the words, "The Five Key Principles of Life", followed by an outline of the principles, "Connect to Your Happy, Meditate Your Mantra, Express Yourself Accordingly, Give Darkness up to Light, and Give Your Live."

Then I heard some words that felt somehow outside of these original five key principles. I heard, "Become the Wayshower."

The instant these words landed into my mind marked the beginning of a five-day period of intermittent inner dictation from a multitude of presences who introduced themselves to me as, "We the Angels of Heaven."

The process of receiving this book was simple. I'd wake up in the middle of the night hearing the beginning of a series of short, extraordinary sentences. I would immediately sit up in bed, and from my phone start emailing the short sentences to myself. I did this non-stop for up to three hours each night.

Each morning after I got up, there would be up to twenty emails in my inbox, each containing many short lines of text.

My job was to put these seamless sentences together into concise and comprehensive stanzas of all shapes and sizes, including couplets, tercets, quatrains and cinquains.

During this process, it felt like I was putting the pieces of a jigsaw puzzle together to form each stanza, which in turn became a full poem.

Speaking of stanzas and poems, this book refers to stanzas as "panes", and the full poems as "light-packets."

Outside of the nightly scribing, I also received many streams of thought from the angels during the day. This happened while standing at the kitchen counter, drying my hair, sitting in my car next to the ocean, having coffee at a restaurant, or just sitting still with my journal or laptop in front of me.

Once each light-packet was complete, the title of it would come to me. After scribing 100 light-packets of all shapes and sizes, the book finally felt complete.

Shortly after I sensed that the book was finished, the angels gave me the words that would be used for both the introduction and the back-book cover. It was titled, "Where Did This Book Come From?" Finally, I was given the title of the book, "Let the Love-Light In."

With all the pieces in place, I was holding the whole picture that is now this brilliant book containing "the new codes coming forth to lighten up your load of sorry nights and faulty flights and major overload."

Ironically, I am not a poet and have never had much interest in poetry. Before this divine writing assignment, I felt akin to Lily Tomlin's character in the Grace & Frankie TV series, who said she really didn't like poetry and would rather read her divorce papers.

But something quickly started happening while receiving and reading this incredible material that was being presented in this way. As I began to comprehend the content of what I was reading, and let it penetrate my mind, I started to feel renewed and quietly blown away. In the first light-packet, the angels were indeed spot-on when they said:

> The packets that you read here
> are designed to wake you up
> To release a joy and inner light
> and expand within your cup

I was feeling awakened. I began to feel endless pulses of love-light coming in through the crown of my head, and all I had to do to experience this was relinquish my own immediate thoughts.

We the mighty angels
are here to help you now
Just stop and wait
Incoming pulse of light
through the top of your sweet head

A few of the book's ideas that have made a deep impression on me so far, have been:

- The ego cannot stop you once your path is clearly sought.
- Medicines are not necessary although you think they are. Illness comes about as a result of dark thoughts that cause cells to squeeze and disease to take root. Healing happens through a process of releasing these dark thoughts to the love-light, so we can shift back into the Oneness of sweet and precious health, where your cells will sing and dance free in the light and heal, or shift and purify all toxins of the night.
- Abundance doesn't come from the world, rather it is a heaven-sent delight, a never-ending pulse directed towards us now. Situation changes cannot impede the flow of abundance once your sweet abundance is set up to break the old code of working hard and struggling to make money.

MY PERSONAL OBSERVATIONS ABOUT THIS BOOK

Designed for light workers. This book is designed primarily for those who are consciously choosing to be a light in the world - in whatever way they are electing to do that - and are ready to let go of some inner obstacles that are impeding them from moving fully forward on their path.

> You are here to save the world
> said the shining light so near
> Too brilliant to ignore
> Too happy to despair

And these two panes:

> Ancient codes of wonder
> released onto you
> Releasing inhibitions
> to bring you forth your due
>
> We the mighty angels
> are calling out your name
> to help you with the turmoil
> and step beyond the pain

Many angels coming through this book. In the first light-packet, the angels tell us, "We've gathered all together to heed the ancient call, sit back, enjoy the moment, and let these words befall."

They refer to themselves in many ways throughout the book, including, we the angels of heaven, we the ancient angels, we the mighty angels, we the holy messengers, mighty friends and mighty hosts.

And this pane:

> You're getting it now
> You're seeing that there are many of us
> And as you open up to our sweet love
> you'll see much more than this

Numerous references to the now. The light codes that are coming through this book have the capacity to awaken us to a deep state of present moment awareness. The following is a small sampling of the frequent references to the now that are contained "on pages shining forth."

- When we travel to tomorrow we let love be denied
- Take it in this moment, a moment out of time, and still your mind of all its grind, and let the love-light in
- To be in the flow is not to think of the past
- Stay right here in this moment because that is where the love is

Expounding my own spiritual understanding. As I continued to explore this book, opening each pane and gently heeding its words and the love-light it was transmitting, I had the feeling that part of the reason the angels gave me this writing assignment was due to my current level of understanding of the many spiritual precepts and practices contained herein.

At the same time this book has also enhanced my understanding of the many themes that are incorporated into it, including forgiveness, ego, physical healing and angelic guidance - in ways that are delightful and deeply liberating.

A luminous new toolbox. The more I read this book, the more I saw it as a brand-new toolbox containing a collection of cutting-edge metaphysical tools that were being lovingly presented to us to use. Some of my favorite tools so far have been:

How to manifest abundance:

> When frightened thoughts abound
> which tell you of your lean
> catch them by the tail
> and throw them now back in
>
> You will not be denied
> a livelihood of love
> but fear you must nip off
> like a flower in its bud

How to let go:

> There's nothing I can say to you to make you understand
> It's not my place to do that so I'll open up my hand
> and in love I'll rise above
> the need to make you bend
> and simply settle into love from up above this plane I see

The angels even told us in the last light-packet that now that we have these new tools, use them well.

You have the tools
Now use them
Trust them
Believe in them
They are beyond your way
That's why they work

Companion to A Course in Miracles

As a student of A Course in Miracles for many years, I felt that this book was a fitting companion to The Course, presenting many of the Course's themes in a way that was unique and refreshing.

In relation to the Holy Spirit:

It is your choice when fear crawls up
to quell your spiritual sight
You merely seek beyond the pale
and choose the other Guide

He loves you well and will not fail to bring you back to peace
when you retract your fiery stance to control your destiny

In relation to the illusion of separation:

It's not that we are separate
I AM with you now
You dreamed of pure non-fiction
and made it real somehow

WHERE IS THIS BOOK COMING FROM?

When I asked the angels where this book was coming from they said it was coming from a mighty high-up plane from the angels of the shores of distant planes. These words of distant starry nights. It is coming from a higher part of you, or the Christ Mind. The Mind that has come to save us from the hell of our lower desires, wants and needs.

HOW HAS THIS BOOK AFFECTED ME?

Shortly after the five-day writing process I entered into an accelerated forgiveness phase, in which my own personal blockages and fears were magnified.

This was happening so that some of my false beliefs could come to the surface to be forgiven or released by me. Since the angels have offered new forgiveness tools and high truths by way of this book, this process, although challenging, has also been deeply transformative and healing, as blockages coming up have been quickly sent "to the land of love to be transformed into the light."

It was especially helpful to hear this following message from the Mighties:

> "This is about helping you clear the fear with truth. When blockages are recognized they can only be healed by truth, and we will provide you with the Highest Truth in the moment and it will be up to you to absorb and allow it to heal your mind."

The only messages I've held back from this body of work were detailed guidance messages regarding my future, including some potential happenings the angels say will take place over the coming months. I will be sharing some of this guidance in an upcoming blog, as these events start coming to fruition.

From the moment these angels introduced themselves to me, I have found myself being quickly ushered into a new reality and a new life.

There are truly no words to convey how deeply grateful I am to have been given this material, and how happy I am to do my part in bringing it to those who are meant to read it, in a world that, in the face of current global turmoil and madness, is shifting from darkness to light in a big way.

In many ways the Mighty Angels are still a mystery to me, but what I know for sure is that their love is enormous and their guidance is splendid, and they are coming to us now in many ways on this planet, including through the pages of this book that you're holding. A book filled with 100 light-packets that have been lovingly and brilliantly designed to help guide us back home to the love-light, and to the Mind of God that we've never really left.

Just stay the straight and narrow
and travel through these panes
Open each one quietly
and let it light its flame

Take no thought of how or why
Just gently heed these words
The light from them will do the rest
and softly guide you home

I hope these panes, or portals into mighty high-up planes, have the same effect on you that they are having on me, and

that you love your journey through them as much as I continue
to love mine.

Onward and upward.

With much love-light,

Stefanie

DEDICATION

To all of us who are choosing the love-light.

TABLE OF CONTENTS

WE THE ANGELS OF HEAVEN

We the ancient angels
of love so sweet and strong
are bringing words of ecstasy
of a long-forgotten song

We the mighty angels
are answering to your call
for simple succulent wisdom
to free you from the fall

Take no thought of how or why
Just gently heed these words
The light from them will do the rest
and softly guide you home

It doesn't matter what you've done
or how you view yourself
We bid you now to see your light
and find your inner mirth

The angels now they know you
They know your very heart
You've subscribed to Oneness
much longed for from the start

The packets that you read here
are designed to wake you up
To release a joy and inner light
and expand within your cup

1

We come to you with wisdom
on pages shining forth
We're standing at the precipice
of love's eternal hearth

Just stay the straight and narrow
and travel through these panes
Open each one quietly
and let it light its flame

We the angels of heaven
have come to call you out
from your long night of sacrifice
and deep unyielding drought

We the angels of heaven
are here to fill you now
with love's embrace
and soft white space
to countenance your brow

We've gathered up the harvest
with these mere ancient words
containing all the wisdom
to lay you down your swords

We the mighty angels
We love you from above
We hover here outside your fear
with wings to lift you up

We the holy messengers
are dropping words of light
to open up the segue
to a future oh so bright

We're gathered all together
to heed the ancient call
Sit back, enjoy the moment
and let these words befall

Ancient codes of wonder
released onto you
Releasing inhibitions
to bring you forth your due

We the mighty angels
are calling out your name
to help you with the turmoil
and step beyond the pain

We the angels of heaven
are sending words of light
to penetrate your mind
and waken up your Sight

We the mighty angels
are here to help you now
so come onto the light within
for bliss is here and now!

Here from mighty heavens
and magnificent crystal grids

The angels bright will sing to you
with sparkle on their wings

So let yourself absorb them
and wash over your sweet soul
For we the mighty angels
are here to help you now

THE WAYSHOWER

Standing at the crossroads
Clouded with despair
Rooted in complication
springing forth from fear

You stood in trepidation
There was no way out of here
No way to see tomorrow
through thoughts of deep despair

But standing on the horizon
in a place of warmth and care
there stood a brilliant angel
to guide you out of here

She lit a light in darkness
She told you not to fear
She told you of another way
to make your mind but clear

There is no time but present
to sit with your despair
To cool your jets in silence
and watch them disappear

The light of brilliance standing
Your time to know it near
Don't wait until tomorrow, my child
The time is now and here

5

Fear not said the angel
Her words they were so dear

Fear began to soften, the clutches not so near
as you knew without a single doubt
the light would heal your fear

You are here to save the world
said the shining light so near
Too brilliant to ignore
Too happy to despair

Don't wait until tomorrow
for the time is now and here!

PAIN PUSHES US TO LIGHT

The stories may be different
but the love is all the same
Whatever got you to this moment
can be worth the price of pain

Not that pain is needed
to open us to spiritual sight
but on this journey inward
it can indeed push us to the Light

THE FIRE OF HEAVEN

We're here to change ourselves
from fear to light indeed
To gather up our hatred
and hustle up our needs

We light the fire of heaven
and open up the door
We gather up our embers hot
and place them on the floor

I cannot keep you ember
To light you now must grow
into a child of God you see
Into what's now, and so

You won't regret the effort
you found to find the light
For as it dawns on your sweet mind
the past will but go out

YOUR NEIGHBOUR IS YOURSELF

A chance to call our neighbour
A chance to laugh and soar
We cannot hear our laughter
until we open up the door

We must love one another
and memories of insane
There is no bolder answer
that love cannot contain

Give to all your siblings
Your friends and foes afar
Your light has no conditions
No boundaries does it bar

Once you love another
with deep and dwelling care
the doors and mountains falter
and tumble down so dear

You can hold no grudges
when love's embrace does call
and ignites within your heart
to share with one and all

THE EGO IS A PHANTOM

The ego is a phantom
A wisp of false desire
to take you on a memory fest
a journey of no more

Do not fear the ego
for ego's hold is not
It cannot stop you from your path
once it is clearly sought

DESTINY'S LEDGE OF LIGHT

There on destiny's ledge of light
is brightness waiting for
your mind to change
To accept the truth
of One of love and lore

You cannot see the light of love
when in the pain of past
The light is bright and will not stop
till every thought amass

It's easy when you realize
You are God's Radiant Light
He loves you more than you could know
Just trust with all your might

You cannot fail to find the love
that's buried deep inside
It's hiding nought
Just bring it forth
with your but pure desire

Dark thoughts may come
but they will go
when in the light you live
Soften your eyes
Trust the Lord
and only but forgive

THE WRITER IN OUR MIND

The problem is the author
The writer in our mind
who tells us we are separate
and cannot whole we find

The master of illusion
He cannot keep us bound
We must move up and onward
through the corridors of our mind

And standing at the precipice
of all our false despair
an ancient Hand is waiting
to Lead us out of here

His love and mercy calls us
back to Home we know
This Home our true pasture
and in it do we Glow

This place is not material
as we know it here on earth
It is fantastical and splendid
with crystal grids and mirth

And oh the love that waits for us
We cannot know it now
Yet somewhere deep inside us
we Know it oh so well

The care and love of heaven
It cannot be denied
no matter how we wander
into falsity and lies

The light is here and now, my friend
My brother of the light
So take this journey with me now
for together we'll make it right

Stay not too long in anguish
Sink not too long in fright
The angels they await you
to lessen up your plight

When sink in pain you tarry
and falter on your way
the answer will forever be
in light and love today!

WHY NOW MUST YOU HIDE?

Linger not in darkness
It is not at all for real
It is time to burst illusion
and choose instead to heal

We love you so completely
like the sun and moon combined
Oh travel not into the night
when truth awaits your mind!

FLOWERS OF THE ANGELS

The flowers of the Angels
are blooming for you now
Springing forth from kindness
to soften up your brow

They wither not in darkness
They never die in vain
They're here in brightness always
to alleviate your pain

Their colors are so vibrant
Their scents of wild terrain
No human can explain them
To enjoy them is their aim

Their petals soft and flimsy
Their colors oh so bright
The rain and sun and clouds on earth
will bring them to delight

Fail not to see them standing
in their brightness on the earth
They bloom for you, to sooth your soul
and make you one with mirth

OH BRINGER OF THE CALL

We cannot shake the embers
of yesterday's demise

Until we come to forefront
of love's embracing eyes

We bow our heads in Silence
We give it up with might

Your song of gladness wonder
Your soul of pure delight

We're loved so very deeply
by God of one and all

The time has come my brother
Oh bringer of the Call

PURE OMEGA ONENESS

The pure omega oneness
The Answer to us all
is stifled in the darkness
when we cannot hear its Call

Open up your mind oh dear
and let its faith be known
and do not let your follies
keep you from your Own

THE ESSENCE, SPIRIT BURNING

The essence, spirit burning
Its gladness, its delight
The master of ourSelf
We cannot be denied

Our Father oh he loves us
From this we cannot hide
We cannot be forgotten
We won't be left behind

Sink in pain if you must
but the answer will forever be
that God is not forgotten
in light and love in thee!

YOUR BLANKET WILL APPEAR

The bird of long-forgotten
We cover up our pain
A far too narrow gateway
The silence but remains

Love oh yes the answer
to all your failings here
and in the presence of angels
your blanket will appear

NO TIME BUT THE PRESENT

Take no thought for tomorrow
The time is here and now
Your thoughts of past and future
will crinkle up your brow

They serve no other purpose
but cause you stress and strain
There is no past, your future gone
So welcome in refrain

When we travel to tomorrow
we let love be denied
We cannot know the precious
when the Blazing Light we hide

THE BLAZING LIGHT

The Blazing Light is calling from terrors dark inside

If we will only follow its sacred call from High

Its yonder call awaits us in this moment now

God the Source of Love is bidding you back Home

STEP FORTH INTO THE LIGHT

What come of fright my fellow
when you do understand
that fear is but a folly
A trap to keep you bland

Choose not this false identity
Step forth into the light
You deserve such sense and wonder
of heaven's pure delight

Walk with feet of progress
in sureness, love and light
Who's waiting for you here and now
will light your eyes with Sight

You cannot know the wonder
The precious sense of joy
until the thoughts of ego's vice
are given to Envoy

TO BASK THE STARRY STILL

The stars are out tonight my dear
Into your mind they fall
like sparks of heaven,
falling light
Into your house the candles call

They light your mind
with merry thoughts
and love you can't explain
On inner planes you meditate
and bring them home again

There's nothing like the beauty
of your soul's undying love
and once you wake its godly state
there is no turning back

To feel the love from High Above
is worth whatever it takes
The giving up to your true love
is not a sacrifice

It is the way to joy today
when stars do enter in
to your sweet mind
that opens wide
heavenly parades within

Of love and light
that is so bright
you'll never lone again

The merry are not lonely
for their love is deep inside
They call it forth
and step into a glorious bask abide

Not happy are the ones
who sit in darkness still
But they will come in their own time
to bask the starry still

When they can see
that they can't plan
their life away in vain
They'll surrender to the Father
who'll guide them home again

Trust that He will guide your steps
to further and beyond
What could you know of His Will for you
when you can barely see your hand?

Trust Him now
Table your plans, relax, enjoy the flow
You cannot plan more than He can
for your unfurling show!

THE ABSENCE OF FEAR

The stars of bright almighty are sprinkling on you now
They bright the night with sparks of light
to lighten up your now
You know them well oh please do tell of wonder glory given
To wake your mind with what you find
when in your silence receive them
The glory of a risen mind to His eternal love
The absence of fear in the now and here
is one sweet symptom
of surrendering to and abiding in His oh glorious Love

YOUR PLANS

Give not another thought my dear to small and pitiful plans
Your future is not yours to hold, it is in Mighty Hands

The only thing you need to know is joy is fast at hand
You'll walk along the starry nights on love's far distant lands

You'll walk the beach of distant shores
in waters soft and sands
and wade around in love's embrace to tell of light abound

CRYSTALS

Crystals are a metaphor for heaven's love and light
To touch the gems of this green earth
will bring you pure delight

They are so pure and even love to sparkle in the night
They are from love and light you see
so hold them nice and tight

Even though they can't compare to ones at heaven's site
Love them well and use them in your meditation lore
for they alleviate the fear and help you love amore

JESUS

Jesus is our brother, our shining light of love
He cannot wait to show us the love from up above
He wants you more than ever now to soften up your load
so he can penetrate your mind and help you grow abroad

Will you join him now my brother, oh lover of the light?
And help bring forth God's pure love
to your brothers of the night?
Jesus was not religious in the way they tried to prove
His message was so simple: That we are from pure Love!

CRYSTAL WATERS

Drink the crystal waters for they will help restore
the memories of oneness in memory banks yet stowed

Water is a conductor of frequency and light
You may not know how much it helps
So sip and drink delight

Water helps you focus on this very moment grand
and bring you back to wonder, to the merriment at hand

MY BROTHER OF THE LIGHT

You are my brother holy
no matter how you see
yourself unkempt and wallowing
in the mirror held to ye

You cannot see your light as yet
but this I know for sure
That you are one with heaven's song
while you tarry on the floor

As you still yourself a moment
and let the love awake
you might just feel
how much you're loved
right now and feel the quake!

GRATITUDE TO GOD

God a holy deity
Yet you are part of me
To show up bright in my small mind
has meant the world to me

A long road I have travelled
on grounds unsure and bleak
But all along you waited
for my time to drop the seek

I know it's all a dream
I haven't left your Mind
And yet I'm filled with wonder
that finally You I find!

MESSAGE FROM THE ONENESS

It's not that we are separate
I AM with you now
You dreamed of pure non-fiction
and made it real somehow

The time has come though rightly
to understand the truth
To break off is impossible
It's just a silly ruse

To separate from Oneness
A fantasy, a lie
So wake in One you Holy Son
and take your place on High

THE SUN IS IN YOU NOW

Take no thought for tomorrow
The sun is in you now
Sit up tall
Heed the call
and know your Glorious Oneness!

TAKE A STAND ON LOVE TODAY

Spirit oh so bright has come to take me home
it travels down my spine and brightens up my throne

Love is not so bright when we falter on our own

The most difficult thing we can do is love ourselves

Yes-no yes-no. There's like a push-pull, push-pull.

And sometimes we don't know what to do with ourselves

You don't have to do anything other than love yourself

Right there across the horizon of time
there's a vessel of love coming right towards you

Come what may but hold fast to thine own self be true

Stargazing across distant horizons is
the way today to find yourself

Don't despair
Be aware in this moment grand and
you will see all is perfectly well
Take a stand today and you will find your house of cards
crumbling into a wall of love

Take a stand on love today

YOUR REWARD

There is no need to wonder now about all these trivial things
Like what to eat, put on your feet

Your needs are surely met
You will be lovingly held in God's good grace
and abundant love

Take no thought of your reward for yours is sure indeed
For trinkets, coins and plastic cards cannot fulfill your needs

Love will fall like alcohol to fill you to the brim
You will not think you have to drink to sustain a happy grin

The joy you feel will be so real that all the foolish thoughts
will leave you fast forward blast to take your message High
to grounds of light where soaks delight
in sunny basking skies

Blue birds sing and on their wing a call of ancient praise
will raise you high and sing your love to whistle in the wind

The wind it calls you far above to hear your ancient name

You cannot know how much you're loved
until you drop the pain
and open up to your sweet Self who waits in Radiance

Do not wait or hesitate to claim what is but yours
The wings of praise they raise you up to love's undying call

For your reward is calling now to joy now you must go
to stake your claim don't hesitate just glisten in the now

THE BLUE BIRD OF HAPPINESS

Just look at him
How sweet
The blue bird of happiness
He's everywhere
When you open your eyes and listen
He'll be there
Egging you on
Into the wonder of You
Into the wonder of love
Of life
Listen
Watch
You'll see

GOD'S GUIDE

The faulty holes you stumble down are caverns in the mind
They cannot trip you anymore and cause you to be blind
You have to choose another way than stepping into hell

It is your choice when fear crawls up
to quell your spiritual sight
You merely seek beyond the pale
and choose the other Guide

He loves you well and will not fail to bring you back to peace
when you retract your fiery stance to control your destiny

God's Guide appears and takes your hand
to lead you out of fear

Just listen and allow him to replace your fear with love
The answer is surrender and softly drop the glove

LOVE'S UNDYING EMBERS

Love's undying embers
are waking in you now

Wake up and see the glory be
when thoughts of false rapport
They flicker fore
They fall away
and though they stay
you cannot hear them more

Your attention now is on the way
to love's enduring brace
You cannot hold your focus
on what no longer serves you well

And now you know that you must go
for now it is the time
They call you from the crystal grid
and frequencies of high

Oh God the joy that I know now
is sparkling, standing tall

COLORS AND CRYSTALS OF HEAVEN

The gems and cutting edges
They sparkle in the sun
Perfection in the moment
The colors are so fun

The lovely beads of water
that dance on heavens door
will soften up the edges
and restore your mind to yore

The colors oh so vibrant
They cannot be described
They decorate the dawn
with pastel hues and tides

Of blue to welcome in the morn
The crystal grid of heaven
is calling to you now
to seek and be and leaven

When heaven comes a calling
which can quite happen now
You enter into magic
A state of love and glow

This world is but a shadow
of what love has in store
To be embraced

and well encased
in front of heaven's door

Heaven's door does not deny
the ones who want It now
As heaven is a state of mind
A glorious loving Thought

Heaven's gate represents a state
that is our golden chance
to have and hold God's love and grace
which settles on us now

HEAVEN'S GATE

Heaven's gate is not a gate that holds the bar to love
It's open wide to anyone who's bold enough to stride
into the love and stop the flow of all lower thoughts
and take a chance on love today

So rise above the fray of time and ask for your birthright

SONG OF LOVE

I sing to you my song of love
from on that place on high
Your weathered hands, your beaten brow
They are not happenstance

Your tarried way oh brother
It's not the way of love
You cannot know the peace of mind
that comes from letting go

So drop the oars and flow instead
It's simple when you see
that love it cannot be controlled
by you or me or we

THE RIVER

Take me to the river
on this starry night
Feed me to your waters
that I may hypnotize

My needs and wants and all concerns
are washed away pray tell
so I will be prepared
that I may serve you well

Take me to your waters
Cleanse my destiny
so love in me will dwell
and I will freely be Me

ABUNDANCE IS A GIFT

Abundance is a gift sent to you from High
not to be denied with fears of lack and lean
Abundance is a flow sent from way beyond
Your rightly gifts of love will travel forth to you
on wings of mighty doves

ABUNDANCE ALL AROUND YOU

Abundance all around you
It's easy when you see
that God's good gifts surround us
with Gifts eternally

Abundance is a gift
sent to you from Height
A never-ending pulse
A heaven-sent delight

Understanding is not needed
to open up this lane
on which the gifts from heaven
will reach you on this day

Open up the channels
in your tired and weary mind
Do not block it now
with fears that lack and bind

Your money is not wanting
Nor will it be again
once you clear this channel
from thoughts of lack and lean

It requires that you are conscious
and stop them in their flow
so peace becomes the alternate route
on which it finds you now

46

Free your mind of worries
Throw away your fears
and money will travel forth to you
on wings of mighty doves

Hard labour and strife
will not abundance last
They are old and stale ideas
rooted in the past

Abundance is a flow
sent from way beyond
Open up the pathways
and treasures will abound

We do not have to wait
for morrow on the ridge
to have the gifts of heaven
that come to us abridge

It's okay to call it money
Money is not what's bad
It's the thoughts and fears
that surround that fare
that makes us all so sad

Your money is not wanting
Nor will it be again
once you clear this channel
directed to you now

Money will delight
On this you can be sure
Sit within the wonder
It's coming now it's here!

DRIVE IS NOT THE WORD

Drive is not the word
for what is in me now
It's an opening to the Oneness
of peace and flow and how

THE LIGHT HAS COME

The light has come to you my child
It's written on your face
I've loved you long with one sweet song
that now you have embraced

See how it all changes
when you open yourself wide?
Have fun my child
Enjoy this light
For this you've long since strived

Oh happy is your future
filled with God's embrace
Of angels lighting up your mind
so you can share this place

On shores of grace, a happy space
You'll live the happy dance
Onward upward
Sure delight
Your heaven will enhance

Have fun my child
Enjoy the light
for this you so deserve
There is no time but presence
to live and love with verve!

NATURE IS A CALLING

In summer do we wallow
on shores of pure delight
To bask in glowing sunshine
To stretch our limbs to light
Oh tarry not in darkness
in front of TV sets
When nature is a calling
oh lets oh lets oh lets

DISAPPOINTMENT IS A SHAM

Disappoint is a sham
An excuse to withhold your love
A grievance to be released
Forgive your disappointment
and realize they were doing the best they could

HOW LONG WILL YOU TARRY?

Will you tarry longer
and strengthen up your might?
Or open up your petals and
let in God's love-light?

The way of strain and struggle
is not the way of flight
It ceases up your cockles
and suffocates your light

Now the time has come
to soften up your stance
Pull back now
Let it go
and join in life's light dance

TRUTH IS SIMPLE

Truth is but so simple
It shines into your mind
from vast arrays of heaven
It beams onto the kind

It only takes awareness
and a choosing of the mind
to let go of petty thoughts
that hamper up and bind

BRIGHT STARS ARE CALLING

Bright stars they are calling
and you are listening well
Just flow with your attention
and tap into the well

We'll shower you with goodness
and joy will fill your mind
and all you need to do is clear
the cobwebs that you find

HEAVEN'S HOLD

Heaven's hold on my small mind
has grown it like a tree
The branches grow where love's sunshine
is calling onto me

The earth of time has grounded me
and done me oh so well
So now expand beyond the land
of this duality

The time has come for me to grow
into the light of love
A fond farewell to those I knew
who loved me as that hand

Grieve not my friend
for I am gone
to soar in distant lands
The time will come when we will see
each other's eyes again
and love's embrace will fall like lace
into our mind again

ABUNDANCE BREAKS THE CODE

When frightened thoughts abound
which tell you of your lean
catch them by the tail
and throw them now back in

You will not be denied
a livelihood of love
but fear you must nip off
like a flower in its bud

Extract it like a splinter
Remove it from your mind
This will get much easier
when practiced over time

Situation changes
cannot impede the flow
of your sweet abundance
set up to break the code

It's okay to want abundance
It is your very right
Abundance breaks the code of fear
and brings it now and here

CRACKING THE MONEY CODES

The principle is simple
The faith now that is hard
especially when your mind
is telling you, you can't

When your bank account tells you
you have no money now
instead of inter-fearing
go to God somehow
This takes light and courage
but it can be done watch how!

You'll find your way to Oneness
You'll do it, yes you can
and as you shift from fear to love
a miracle will land

When the miracle on the inside
reflects the one without
you will happily know
and there will be no doubt

So banish all your thoughts
of lack and lean and fear
and money will infill your life
to drench your now and here

MY ABUNDANCE LIES IN ME

My abundance lies in me
There is no source out there

Release the treasures darling
Unlock the codes of fear

And love, your real inheritance
will brighten up your mind

Your inheritance it will find you
Of this you can be sure

Falter not in thoughts of nought
and rise to meet your needs

THE GIFT

The gift it's going to be there
Of this you can be sure
Just open up the gateway
Open up the door

MEDICINES ARE NOT NEEDED

The medicines are not needed but
though you think they are

Back into Oneness within its sweet and precious health
Falter not in this regard and alignment will be true

And in this shift your cells will sing and dance free in the light
The cells they shift and purify all toxins of the night

When your dark thoughts caused them to squeeze
and this disease took root

But now take heart and purify the thoughts, that's all you do
And it's easy once you know that it's not you,
it's Me that takes your thoughts away

You my dear just leave them here and I will Do the rest
Let your mind and body serve me, I will do the rest

Oh the joy you'll feel when you do heal
in this powerful and loving way
and long since when the power of
Zen begins this starry flight

So don't prolong your journey here
right here between your eyes

If you only knew what's coming to you
you'd drop the pressure now

Don't delay bring forth today the ancient diamond hue
Because you gave your mind to Him
and heard the ancient call

DIAMONDS ARE FOREVER

Your life is like a diamond
Turn in and see it now
The colors in the corners
A pinpoint into now

We cannot know this glory
from tired and weary eyes
What takes us back to oneness
that's only found inside

But how you ask
do I invite
this presence of the light?

By wanting It
more than this fight
for rigid thin control

But oh if you could only see
the power of letting go

The diamond Mind
it will arouse your senses inner true
of love and light and intense fire
of propagating hues

This new life of wonder
I do not have a clue

Yet somewhere in my mind
I know I've given it to you

Of this I will not falter
for I can only gain
your love and peace and exquisite ease
that comes from letting go

And all it took was that little choice
in all those moments
when I subsided
and opened to your loveliness afoot

I feel it now oh the sweet flight
of surrendering to the light

ANCIENT WINGS OF LIGHT

Ancient wings of light are calling to me now
Once the gateway opens the love won't be denied
You've settled into Oneness and let the fear subside

In that love-light diamonds will fall like peppermints
into your mind with one of a kind flowers for your soul

The flow is flowing and that's all you need to know

Rest your head now traveller, traveller of the light
Lay back onto your pillow and have a lovely flight

We'll be here to re-greet you in the morning light

We love you and will be here with messages to delight
So bask now in the stillness and energize your brain
so we can reveal the wonders of the Universal Mind

Good night lay down be merry on your way
We got it covered and now go back to sleep!

HOW SWEET THE SOUND OF ANGELS

Don't falter now stay with us
and discern what's ours from yours
And together we'll bring a rich white gleen
to minds who join the chorus

SPIRITUAL LOVE IS CALLING

Spiritual love is calling
It's not the love of land
It's above the fray of lower thoughts
that bind your mind to bland

The message it is simple
Just release your mind to All
and love's sure way will find you today
and light your mind with ease

Alight to tall with bliss from All
ensures your path from fray

Take it in this moment
A moment out of time
And still your mind of all its grind
and let the love-light in

WILL NOT YOUR MIND SHINE BRIGHT?

To still it now will be worth it, every bit of effort to get there
To get there is how you'll experience the love of God
And is it not sure worth it, is that not what you want?
Or choose instead to bang your head on tables of despair?
Going nowhere on a fast and desperate track?
What will it take to break you of this pattern of hanging on
to false control of your shifting goals and problematic strife?
This is not the way to love's enduring grace
So choose you must
to gain or bust and live your happy dance!

KARMA

The choice is yours my beauty
We love you either way
And your despair will keep you near to earth's unholy ways
of fight and might and all things quite
treacherous by compare
But the other way is calling and calling loud and light
For your destiny is on distant shores
of brightness and lightness
Of love and letting go that don't compare
to strugglesome weary minds
Control it is illusory and cannot help you live
You'll fight the flight or give into the streams of basking still
And on the rivers mighty of your pure peace
you give and you'll see light and spread your
love rather than control your destiny
Control is not the answer although
you've learned that it sure is
In order to release you must want It more than to manipulate
There's no fun in manipulation, its results are up and down
Up in egos realm and down again to tarry to and fro
There's no love in the illusion of this
winning then losing game
There'll be ego fun followed by deep despair
And what will that give you in the end?
Nothing but coming back to this
over and over like a hamster on the wheel
of one sorry situation and then another
Life after the other you'll befall

So release yourself from karma,
even though it's not really real
In your mind it might as well be
as you repeat it now and again
You have to want love fully for it to enter into your mind
but once it does there's no going back
to caverns in your mind

INNER DICTATION

This process is so sweet
To stop and start with your sweet heart
has meant the world to me

A flower it is growing
for all the world to see
Capture fantastical moments
Sit and rest with me

Your flower is so holy
We want you to be free
Just rest now here a while my dear
and leave the nest to me

The key is letting go
into the Mighty Hands
The process it is simple
Let's settle into stillness
and let the rest be yours

LOVE'S FORGOTTEN LANDS

The power is so golden on this lastic land
When ships do sail to yesterday the power is at hand
From powerful mighty shores
Standing at the precipice of awesome distant lands
We're here to serve the mountain groove
of love's forgotten shores
So tally up the scoreboards and soften up your stands
The mountains they seem high
with decorated vans

To wallow in misery
is such a waste of time
For time is not the author
of your sweet melody

And takes what's yours
beyond your chores of tranquility
Why now do you suffer?
Do you not now see
that all is yours to have and hold
with constant certainty?

The method is so simple and if you'll take my hand
I'll take you on a journey to love's forgotten lands

Seek no more your flowers in illusion of the night
Walk with me and you will see that Simple Will delights

FROLIC ON STARRY DISTANT LANDS

Consciousness will follow into the starry nights
Now press away your all that's clay
and meet your just reward

The ego cannot hold up in authoritative grip
when you soften with your own small choice
to further un-eclipsed

The ego doesn't want for you to free your mind
You're on your way to frolic on starry distant lands

THE RAINBOW IN YOUR MIND

You cannot see the wonder of the rainbow in your mind
when you falter in your fear and let it eclipse your mind

Shiny distant shores
of sand and sun so tanned
We see your plight go out like lights
and love to take a stand

It's very simple darling
We'll show you just so how
When recede you do and let us in
to light your way with ease

We've given you the tools
and use them wisely now
They are not hard when love's reward
lights up your mind so bright

This love you see will welcome those
who still suffer in despair
But your mind bright with peace and light
will entice their weary mind

Your brother will see
what God has in store for them
Slowly surely in God's sweet time
which settles on us now

JUST TRAVEL TO THE LIGHT

I am not the one who knows how much your light
will pave the way for those today who
you reach with God's love
It's not yours you see it's fancy free and will not hide its light
for those who choose they cannot
lose to seek and they will find

It doesn't take much effort when you let your mind recede
And once you see what's standing there
in shimmering brilliant Sight
you won't go back oh no for what? Just travel to the light!

DOVES OF LOVE AWAIT YOU NOW

Travel towards the light and we will
Carry you on wings of love
Don't hesitate to leave
Surrender to the top of your head and
you will surely see the love
and light in multitudes on love's forgotten shores
Come round right now and feel the love
from which your path be shown
Just pull back your thoughts and bring
your attention to that place
that you now know with effort spent
It's easy now so continue now to watch the All expand
My God what love when you do yield
to the place above your head
The doves of love await you now and here
It's so simple girl just do it now!

RECEDE NOW INTO THE ONENESS

Recede now into the oneness
to that place above your head
Bring your full attention up above the nose
and settle into a Oneness that this world will never know
You know now how to do it
So do not linger long
in thoughts of pain and emotional gain
Choose instead your peace within
It is so beautiful you know now what I mean

Share this light by being there
The rest won't even matter
Every time the fear arouses you
and takes over your mind to row
just tell it to surrender and your job is to take the place
in the middle of your brow

It's not going to matter what's happening out there
Your peace within will not refrain to find you now
and light your mind with God's refrain
All else will matter no
Just try at ANY time
Let love infill your mind
The rest will follow from there

IT'S NOT UP TO YOU WHAT THEY DO

It's not up to you what they now do
when your job is to love

You cannot control what they say and do
and it will matter not
when love's embrace lights up your mind
you'll have no need in That
And love will befall those in your life
in a new and sweetly way

So don't despair we'll show you where
when you've forgotten on the way

NOT ALL WILL COME THIS WAY AND THAT'S OKAY

This place that you are going
Not all will come this way
It's not up to you to encourage one
who is not prepared or interested at the time
Just leave alone and be on your way
to love within your mind

You're not here to change anyone's mind
They must do that in their sweet time
Your job is so simple
You'll know just what to do
So never sweat when things seem dark
Just let them merely be
And you go back to the diamond in your Mind
It's all somehow so right here now that matter anything not

In times of fear you must obey this law of love
and your will go in leaps and bounds

Travel not alone cause we're here to help
from the place where power abides
From awesome cups of brilliant love
and angels of mighty wings

HEAVEN'S HELPERS

We're here to help you now
And now you know that's true together
And because of that
there's no turning back
There's nothing we can't do!

ANGELIC HELP

You can't imagine the love that's surely here and now
when you open up and fill your cup
with the love from us today
You're getting it now
You're seeing that there are many of us
And as you open up to our sweet love
you'll see much more than this
We're here to help you in every way
so open up and ask! Okay!

YOUR WORK IS JUST BEGINNING

From the mighty wings of angels onto your local shores
You'll dance and sing quite merrily
and bask in the sweet sun
We're so happy that you've opened up to us
Feel the love now my dear
Let it in. Bask in it. Work with it. Whirl with it.
You can handle it now
Your work is just beginning
And it's real light work not some shallow fantasy
Don't look for love rather bask in it
All your opportunities will come to you

STAY CALM AND LEAN

Stay calm and lean. Do the work merrily. You know the rewards. You don't have to be perfect that's why we love you so much. Now love yourself too. Do your best we'll do the rest. Chill out now. We'll be there for everyone we send you to. Everyone else just be the love to. So all bases are covered.

WE'LL HELP YOU WIT THE WORDS

We'll help you wit the words. Just bask into the love.
All else is plain as day. We are having fun with you
now because we can see how open you're becoming.
Not all channels want to be used for God's plan. They
resist it and strive to go against it with all their merry
might. You don't even have to think about that.

THE REST WILL FOLLOW

Don't bother feeling bad. Just learn and
do your best. The rest will follow.

OUR NEW RELATIONSHIP

How you are seeing when you're looking at the world is a deep distortion. That is why you need help. But you don't think you need help, that is why you do need it. The questions will come to you. Just let them come as well. You're settling in our new relationship and that is good. You're really wanting it which is really good. Just settle into it and we'll take care of everything.

All is well in All of creation

EGOS ROUGH WILL FLOURISH

Egos rough will flourish
But they will fade away too

For the light of love that stands here now
will overcome that thought

Be not swayed when they erupt
like firecrackers in the night

NERVOUSNESS

Nervousness is a place you go to hide yourself
To build up all the walls and keep your light out

The key to this strong stance is to settle into Self
and choose that very place that will free you from that knot

Feel the storm around you but choose not to succumb
Instead fall back, get back on track
and breathe the Answer wide

It's all okay no matter what

TRAVEL NOW IN STILLNESS

Travel now in stillness
to love's forgotten shores
Go back into the light of love
and choose that now instead

HOW TO FORGIVE

Release it to the beam
A direct tunnel to the love
Just pick it forth and with hands up let it go with delight
to the land of love to be transformed into the light
You'll feel it go into the pipe of light
that is surrounding you now
It's easy when you realize how easy it is!

THE IMAGINARY TUNNEL IS REAL

Celebrate the oneness from these far distant shores
Let's rally up the darkness of twilight's dark chagrin
and place it at the mouth of the imaginary tunnel

It's not imaginary, oh no, it's real
but for your purposes right now it feels imaginary
until you feel the results of letting the dark thoughts go into it
Just do it, yes you can
And as you keep doing it you will feel the relief of doing it
You will know it is real
Just do it
Nip it in the bud and do it!

MANIFESTING IN LOVE

Rest in God's love
Now open up to Him
That's all you do the rest will come to you
And the love will be all you want and need
And in that love all sweet things will come to pass

HOW TO FORGIVE YOUR BROTHER

When a brother comes to mind
send them oh the light
Do not keep your weary thoughts of
their plight that irritate your mind
Just pluck it out and you will find the overall this left behind
It's easy when you want the love instead of doubt

PEACE WILL COME

You have to want it fully
In this you can be sure
that peace will come
Share its spell
on ancient distant days

THE SHORES OF DIAMOND MIND

There is no past or future in a mind that's filled with love
And you will know when oh so sure your
Thoughts are now and here
You won't have to collect your thoughts of low
because you won't want them anymore
And soar with angels bow
and here to the shores of distant land
Isn't this so fun
When we frolic in the Sands
and bask and play in love's sweet sands of love today?

The place is not a physical site to which you'll travel afoot
It's here today in your sweet mind just let it come unfold
The scenes of sweet and oh the love
on the shores of diamond mind

A COURSE IN MIRACLES

A Course in Miracles indeed
It tells of love not pain
It answers us in Oneness
in which we will remain

No matter thoughts of separate
that cause you constant fear
There is no thought of Oneness
when we do but see near

In thoughts of Oneness standing
we celebrate our gain
and let go at long last
of our past and present pain

We cannot know the love of One
until we drop our will
and settle into stillness
from whence the Voice does fill

The Course is breaking the barriers
of ego's final fight
and breaks the band of sinners
who thought that was their plight

There's no such thing as sin
we find out oh so last
There's only love and wonder
Thank God it's come at last!

LETTING GO

There's nothing I can say to you to make you understand
It's not my place to do that so I'll open up my hand
and in love I'll rise above
the need to make you bend
and simply settle into love from up above this plane I see

THE EGO IS A TRICKSTER

The ego is a trickster, a blanket of despair
It doesn't care about you, it revels in your fear
It tries to take your love, and turn it into fear

Fear not said the angel, from out beyond this veil
You cannot know the wonder on the glorious plane
until you stop it in its tracks and choose love once again

THE EGO CANNOT STOP YOU

The ego cannot stop you
although it seems to fill
your mind with fearful thoughts
or memories that chill

The key to freeing Self
from ego's cold vice grips
is place your attention on the love
and let it fall away

CHAKRAS OF DELIGHT

Chakras of delight
are here to serve you now
when we let the love-light in
somewhere somehow right now

Chakras of delight
Flowing like a stream
Travel way from yesterday
in heavens parlor dream

MEDITATION

Meditation it is easy
when all you want is love
The method is so simple
Tune in to what's above

The songs of ancient waiting
The peaceful caressing hues
They are but right there calling
to show themselves to you

Oh don't wait one more minute
to stop, get starry eyed
and usher in the Oneness
that will you then abide

THE GAP OF LOVE

Shift from the gap where God is not
to the gap where God is
It's easy when all you want is love
It's easy when you realize how easy it is!

All the answers are there in the gap of love
All you have to do is want It more than anything else
It's easy when it's REALized
You've got it now

IT'S ALL IN MIGHTY HANDS

When thoughts of deep despair
travel through your mind
Codes that bind the mind
Codes are laws of ego
Laws set up to bind the mind

This causes that or because of that
are clearly forth defined
Bind the mind to this reality in the mind

We cannot break this code and let love in

If we are to break the code
of ancient and of might
we must rise high into stillness
and let love far a flight

Into our minds it lands
from starry distant shores
to bring forth the New Plans
from forth our Mighty Hosts

We'll see it in the wonder
These new laws they'll surround
Infill you with happiness and your fare
Riches in the moment of this so now be sure
When or where will not you care
It's all in Mighty Hands

THE CRYSTAL GRIDS OF HEAVEN

The crystal grids of heaven are coming to you now
to free you from the headspace of fear and lack and no

The crystal grids of heaven are calling to you now
The crystal grids are calling you back home

The crystal grids of heaven are calling forth your light
to light your brother's pathway that darken up the night

The crystal grids of heaven are here to bring you Home
to the place you never left

The crystal grids of heaven are calling you from fright
so open up the pathways and find your way to Sight

The crystal grids of heaven are calling you from the night
to release the hold of ego and step into the light

YIELD INTO THE NOW

Release your brow to ancient tones of love and crystals high
It's so simple and so easy, just yield into the now
Be pulled by love from up above and let yourself be free

OPEN UP, LET IT IN

It's always about love
It's never not about love
How could it not be about love
When everything IS love

Open up, let it in
and witness the unfolding
of love's glorious dance
of creation's calling
Riches abound
Be still now
You can do it
In this moment
Let the love-light in
and dance the dance
that is being
Played for you now

YOUR MIGHTY GUIDE

I'm here with you now
I am your mighty guide
You can ask me anything
I am always here

I never leave your side
I love you so much
That you'll never really know
until you drop you

WE THE MIGHTY ANGELS

We the mighty angels
are dancing with you now
with heaven's grace to befall your face
in love's sweet nectar flow

You asked for perfect Oneness
See how fast it falls?
When you understand
you can't contain
the love of Mighty Friends

You'll learn to let it grow
from seed to morrow's tree
All happening now
with one sweet bough
in grassy eternity

The meadows of tomorrow
They're with you oh right now
with soft embrace to meditate
on grassy luscious moor

Do not waste a minute in any day to come
for words to wait and love to fate
your welcoming succumb

The world it needs your wonder
Your light from God above

Let it flow, rock its tow
Journey on towards the light

Your brothers now do need you
So soften up your stance
Do let love in and share it well
in every circumstance

We the mighty angels
are here to help you now
Just stop and wait,
incoming pulse of light
through the top of your sweet head

Don't wait another minute
for you can have it now
We love you with hearts overflowing
and will dance your dance here now!

LET THE LOVE-LIGHT IN

I'm so happy with this love
that's found me here today
I want to share it now with you
because it's impossible to contain
There is something sweetly happening
It cannot be explained
with words of light even dynamite
but a feeling in the mind
Open now to splendor
Let the love-light in
You can only know this precious glow
when we drop the trite chagrin
The gate has opened wide
and now the fun begins
There's nothing to do except just be you
and let your love-light flow
Onwards upwards now take flight
and open up to love

DABBLE OR DO

Doing is for those who want it
more than merely dabbling with it
Get out of the way today
There is no other time
than this moment
to enter into wonder,
to enter into stillness
and See what happens

NOW IS THE TIME

Let's take this now
and be on our way
to inner planes and meditate
to abundant distant shores

Now is the time
You do not have to wait
Just call
the ancient song right here today
and put in place these codes
That's all that's required

Wait not another minute
basking in the past

The rest is up to you

You have the tools
Now use them
Trust them
Believe in them
They are beyond your way
That's why they work

Doubt not today
Sit in the wonder of it all
and watch how your life unfolds
like a glorious book written for you
by you and in you

We love you and are with you always

TODAY YOU'LL HAVE IT ALL

Love and light is on the way
to your sweet mind this very day
You have the tools to use to soften up your stance
and brighten up your hues
Much love and laughter finds and penetrates your glance
when all you want is silence to replace the things of bland
You are a mighty creature
Part of God's most glorious dance
So soften up your thoughts of lack
and today you'll have it ALL

YOUR NEW GO-TO

Go to the over-arching reality
Nothing else is pertinent
When you experience the joy of this golden globe beyond
you will find everything you're looking for without looking

Reach high today into skies of blue
and you will see much beyond the horizon
You know this well so strive today to look away
from swells of gray and dark thoughts
Stretch your limbs to love
and you will have it all
Let this be your new go-to

Stay right here in this moment because
that is where the love is

ABOUT THE AUTHOR

Stefanie is a Spiritual Author and Speaker who has dedicated her life to the Great Awakening that is now taking place on this planet. She has a Bachelor of Arts degree from Memorial University of Newfoundland, and is an Ordained Minister of A Course in Miracles. She was awarded the YMCA Peace Medal for her work as a spiritual leader in the community. She currently resides in Paradise, Newfoundland, next to Angels Road. Go figure.

To invite Stefanie to speak at your event, or to sign up for her emails - go to www.stefaniefinn.com

Printed in Great Britain
by Amazon